Chronicles of AWS Summit Ottawa 2022

Compendium of Voices, Reflections, Learnings, and Trends in Cloud Computing Community and AWS

Jonathan Lalou

Chronicles of AWS Summit Ottawa 2022 | Compendium of Voices, Reflections, Learnings, and Trends in Cloud Computing Community and AWS

Copyright © 2022, 2024, 2025 SayaSoft Publishing

First edition: December 2022
Second edition: January 2024
Third edition: May 2025
Published by SayaSoft Publishing Ltd.
https://www.sayasoft.fr
Cover Image by Jonathan Lalou

About the author

Jonathan Lalou is a highly accomplished technology leader with over two decades of experience architecting and developing complex software solutions. A graduate of Ecole Nationale Superieure des Mines de Nancy with a Master's Degree in Computer Science, he brings a strong foundation in computer science principles to his work. Notably, his career includes several experiences in top management positions, having started as a CTO shortly after graduating and serving as CTO or CTO Deputy three times in his intensive career. His experience spans companies like Sungard, StepInfo / Talan, Paymentus, HSBC, and BNP-Paribas, showcasing his expertise in a wide range of technologies, including Java/JEE, Agile methodologies, and cloud computing. This extensive technical background, combined with his significant leadership experience and the many hours he spent training his teams, makes him a reliable author and tutor for those who can attend his lectures, as well as for those who follow his blog and X (formerly known as Twitter).

To follow the author:
- Blog: http://jonathan.lalou.free.fr
- LinkedIn:
  https://www.linkedin.com/in/jonathanlalou/
- StackOverflow:
  https://stackoverflow.com/users/5804915/jonathan-lalou
- GitHub: https://github.com/JonathanLalou
- Twitter: https://x.com/John_the_Cowboy

By the same author:
- Apache Maven Dependency Management, 2013, Packt, ISBN 978-1783283019
- Application Development with Maven, 2015, Packt, ISBN 978-1783286101
- CTO Compass: a Guide for New CTOs, 2025, SayaSoft Publishing, ISBN 979-8280696945
- Finance for Software Developers, 2023-2025, SayaSoft Publishing, ISBN 979-8281270113
- Chronicles of PyData Paris 2024 | Compendium of Voices, Reflections, Learnings, and Trends in Modern Python Data Science, 2023-2025, SayaSoft Publishing, ISBN 979-8282208375 (also available in French)

Table of Content

Foreword

Disclaimer: Neither the author nor the publisher are affiliated with or represent Amazon, AWS or any of their entities. This publication is an independent work intended to share insights and foster learning within the broader data science community.

📖 Foreword

It is with genuine excitement and heartfelt pride that we present this book — *Chronicles of AWS Summit Ottawa 2022*, inspired by the AWS Summit Ottawa 2022.

This work is more than a simple recap or conference proceedings. It is a curated, reflective, and practitioner-friendly companion designed to help you absorb the real-world strategies, technical patterns, and cultural shifts that define modern cloud architecture. Our goal was to take the energy, expertise, and innovation shared at the summit and distill it into a format that informs, inspires, and lasts.

Over the years, we've seen cloud technology grow from a disruptive innovation into a cornerstone of digital transformation — not just in startups and big tech, but increasingly in mission-critical services, public infrastructure, and citizen-facing platforms. The AWS Summit Ottawa 2022 reflected this maturation with clarity and conviction, showcasing how Canadian organizations are shaping the future of cloud with resilience, creativity, and purpose.

This book is our humble contribution to that evolving story. Whether you're a CTO navigating multi-cloud complexity, a developer eager to sharpen your architectural skills, or a policymaker working on digital strategy, we hope these pages give you tools to act, insights to reflect, and examples to emulate.

We wrote this book with gratitude — for the speakers who shared their journeys, for the engineers building the backbone of tomorrow's internet, and for readers like you who choose to stay curious, critical, and committed to better technology.

Thank you for picking up this book. We sincerely hope it brings you as much value in reading as it brought us in writing.

📖 A Strategic and Technical Companion to the AWS Summit Ottawa 2022

What if you could compress days of expert talks, real-world

case studies, and architectural blueprints from top-tier organizations into one clear, compelling, and actionable book? That's exactly what *Chronicles of AWS Summit Ottawa 2022* offers.

This book captures the most impactful insights shared at **AWS Summit Ottawa 2022**, one of Canada's premier cloud innovation gatherings, and distills them into an easy-to-follow, high-value read — tailored for technology leaders and practitioners alike.

🔍 What's Inside the Book?

- ■ **Deep dives into real AWS use cases** from Canada Life, the CRA, and others — not just what they built, but why and how.
- ■ **Architecture breakdowns** with visuals and plain-English explanations — ideal for both seasoned architects and fast-learning CTOs.
- ■ **Migration and modernization journeys**, including monolith-to-serverless transformations and event-driven refactoring.
- ● **Practical patterns and anti-patterns** in security, scalability, observability, and cost optimization.
- 🕯 **Reflections on DevOps culture, developer enablement**, and the future of cloud infrastructure in the public sector.

⬢ Table of Contents (Sample Program/Menu)

1. **Foreword:** The Cloud at the Crossroads of Innovation and Public Trust
2. **Canada Life Case Study:** Scaling Real-Time Data with Kinesis and Lambda
3. **CRA's Multi-Region Resilience Strategy** with DynamoDB Global Tables
4. **Modernizing Workloads at Scale:** From EC2 to Fargate
5. **Cloud-Native Analytics:** Amazon Athena, Redshift, and QuickSight
6. **Building Secure Architectures:** Zero Trust and IAM Fine-Tuning
7. **Operational Excellence:** Observability, Incident Response, and Chaos Engineering
8. **Leadership Insights:** Cloud Strategy for Government and Enterprises

9. **Final Reflections:** Innovation, Compliance, and Human-Centered Tech

---

📌 Why Read This Book?

- 🔴 **Condensed Wisdom:** Learn in hours what took leading teams years to master.
- ⚫ **Local Relevance, Global Application:** Based on Canadian use cases, but universally applicable to any organization using AWS.
- 🛠 **Toolkit for Leaders:** Whether you're building a cloud roadmap or coaching dev teams, this book gives you the vocabulary, vision, and validation you need.
- 🧩 **Perfect for Decision-Makers:** Not just tech, but strategy — helps bridge the gap between developers and executives.

⚫ Who Should Read This?

- **CTOs** and **Cloud Architects** defining future-proof infrastructures.
- **Engineering Managers** and **DevOps Leads** navigating scalability, resilience, and migration challenges.
- **Public Sector Technologists** delivering secure and citizen-centric digital services.
- **Consultants & SREs** looking for repeatable blueprints for cloud transformation.

🛒 Available Now – Don't Miss Out

If you couldn't attend the summit — or even if you did — this book is your ultimate recap and reference guide. With actionable insights, and critical commentary, *Chronicles of AWS Summit Ottawa 2022* belongs on every tech leader's bookshelf.

Thank you in advance for your trust and curiosity. Please don't hesitate to reach out if you have feedback, reflections, or just want to talk about AWS or cloud computing.

Disaster Recovery and Data Residency in Canada

At the AWS Summit Ottawa 2022, Bill Olsen, Principal Security Leader at Amazon Web Services (AWS), and Scott Levac, Director of Cloud Oversight and Core Technology at the Treasury Board Secretariat, delivered a compelling 43-minute session on disaster recovery (DR) and data residency in Canada. This presentation explored strategies for designing resilient cloud architectures while addressing Canadian data localization requirements. With a focus on balancing availability, cost, and compliance, Bill and Scott provided actionable insights for public sector organizations. Below, we unpack the key themes, enriched with context from the lecture and AWS's mission to deliver secure, scalable cloud solutions.

Business Continuity in the Cloud Era

Bill and Scott framed disaster recovery as a cornerstone of business continuity, particularly in the context of disruptions like the global pandemic. Scott highlighted how the crisis forced Canadian government agencies to adapt swiftly, deploying cloud-based services such as contact centers and mobile apps for vaccine status tracking. This agility underscored the cloud's ability to scale rapidly, contrasting with traditional IT systems hindered by entrenched biases toward on-premises solutions. Scott challenged the notion that legacy systems are inherently safer, noting their limitations during the pandemic.

The session introduced a critical trade-off: the cost of minimizing outages versus the impact of prolonged disruptions. Scott presented a graph illustrating the exponential cost of achieving near-perfect availability against the rising cost of outages, especially in the public sector where reputational damage can escalate to parliamentary scrutiny. Bill emphasized that resiliency and security are intertwined, requiring ongoing efforts to identify and mitigate failure points. This synergy is vital for organizations aiming to maintain trust and operational continuity.

Navigating Canadian Data Residency

Data residency emerged as a pivotal topic, given Canada's stringent requirements for government data. Scott traced the evolution of Canada's data residency policy, which shifted from a restrictive 2017 stance to a risk-based approach in 2019. This change allows departmental CIOs to make informed decisions about storing data outside Canada, balancing security needs with operational realities. Guidelines in Section 4.4 of the Government of Canada's *Guideline on Service and Digital* provide criteria for these decisions, empowering agencies to assess risks based on their specific contexts.

Bill complemented this by discussing AWS's infrastructure in Canada, including the Canada (Central) Region near Montreal and the upcoming Calgary Region, set to launch in Q4 2023. With an investment of $21 billion over 15 years, the Calgary Region will enhance Canada's cloud capacity, supporting western workloads and leveraging clean energy to reduce environmental impact. This infrastructure ensures compliance with Canadian regulations while offering robust disaster recovery options through multiple availability zones (AZs).

Strategies for Resilient Architectures

The session outlined four disaster recovery strategies—backup and restore, pilot light, warm standby, and hot standby—each balancing complexity, cost, and recovery time. Bill explained that backup and restore suits data loss mitigation, while pilot light maintains core infrastructure for quick activation. Warm standby offers a fully functional, scaled-down environment, and hot standby (active-active or active-passive) minimizes recovery time but increases complexity. A graphic from an AWS blog illustrated trade-offs in design complexity, operational effort, and environmental impact, with Scott noting the cloud's low upfront costs and provisioning agility as key differentiators.

Bill stressed the importance of defining recovery point objectives (RPOs) and recovery time objectives (RTOs), which determine acceptable data loss and downtime. For mission-critical services, these metrics guide strategy selection, ensuring alignment with business needs. Scott added that cloud agility allows organizations to evolve strategies over time, adapting to changing requirements without the capital-intensive projects typical of traditional IT.

Testing and Chaos Engineering

Testing emerged as a critical component of resiliency. Bill advocated for continuous testing, likening disaster recovery to marathon training: practice is essential for success. He recommended tabletop exercises, AWS Well-Architected reviews, and chaos engineering to uncover vulnerabilities. Chaos engineering, inspired by Netflix's approach of "failing constantly" to avoid failure, involves injecting controlled failures to strengthen systems. AWS's Fault Injection Simulator integrates with CloudWatch to test real-world scenarios, helping organizations identify blind spots in monitoring and recovery processes.

Scott emphasized that resiliency extends beyond technology to include people and processes. Business continuity plans must account for administrator access, network availability, and supplier SLAs. By aligning technical strategies with policy-driven outcomes, organizations can achieve robust, compliant disaster recovery frameworks.

Conclusion

Bill and Scott's session at AWS Summit Ottawa 2022 offered a roadmap for public sector organizations navigating disaster recovery and data residency. By leveraging AWS's infrastructure and adopting agile, outcome-focused strategies, agencies can enhance resiliency while meeting compliance requirements. The cloud's flexibility, coupled with rigorous testing, empowers organizations to adapt to evolving challenges, ensuring continuity in the face of disruption.

Links:

- AWS Summit Ottawa 2022 Video: https://www.youtube.com/watch?v=JlkJLdV7woE
- Government of Canada – Guideline on Service and Digital: https://www.canada.ca/en/government/system/digital-government/guideline-service-digital.html
- AWS Resilience Hub: https://aws.amazon.com/resilience-hub/
- AWS Skill Builder: https://aws.amazon.com/training/

Hashtags: #AWSSummit #DisasterRecovery #DataResidency #CloudComputing #PublicSector #AWS #AmazonWebServices #BillOlsen #ScottLevac #GovernmentofCanada

Enhance Security with the AWS Nitro System

In a 46-minute session at AWS Summit Ottawa 2022, Brian Mycroft, Chief Technologist at Amazon Web Services (AWS), delivered an in-depth exploration of the AWS Nitro System, a transformative technology powering modern Amazon EC2 instances. The Nitro System, comprising custom hardware and a lightweight hypervisor, enhances security and performance, offering robust protection for workloads. Brian's presentation detailed the system's evolution, security features, and impact on cloud innovation, providing valuable insights for organizations prioritizing secure computing.

The Evolution of the Nitro System

Brian traced the Nitro System's origins to AWS's virtualization journey, beginning with the 2006 launch of Amazon EC2 using the Xen Hypervisor. While Xen supported millions of customers, its overhead—consuming up to 30% of host capacity—prompted AWS to rethink virtualization. Initiated in 2012 and launched in 2017 with C5 instances, the Nitro System offloads networking, storage, and management tasks to custom silicon, reducing hypervisor overhead to near zero. This shift delivers near-bare-metal performance, with latency reduced to 9–17 microseconds compared to 30–85 microseconds on Xen-based instances.

The Nitro System's iterative development involved acquiring Annapurna Labs to advance silicon innovation. Today, all new EC2 instances leverage Nitro, ensuring customers benefit from its capabilities without additional configuration. Brian emphasized that Nitro is distinct from Nitro Enclaves, which extend confidential computing for specific use cases.

Security as a Design Principle

Security is the Nitro System's cornerstone, designed to eliminate operator access and ensure workload isolation. Brian highlighted the system's hardware separation, with AWS code running on dedicated Nitro cards, isolated from customer workloads. The Nitro Security Chip, embedded on x86 motherboards, traps I/O to non-volatile storage, preventing unauthorized firmware changes. This enables secure bare-metal instances, a feat unachievable with Xen due to potential motherboard state tampering.

The system's APIs are narrowly defined, lacking mechanisms for logging into hosts or accessing customer data. Transparent, line-rate encryption at 256-bit strength secures data in transit (up to 800 Gbps) and at rest, using ephemeral AES-256 keys for instance storage. The Nitro Trusted Platform Module (TPM) 2.0 further enhances security by providing instance health attestation, ensuring only untampered images boot.

Performance and Innovation

The Nitro System's performance benefits stem from its lightweight hypervisor and custom hardware. By offloading tasks to Nitro cards, AWS achieves near-bare-metal performance, with overhead less than 1%. Brian noted significant latency improvements, particularly with Graviton processors, which reduce latency to around 5 microseconds. Nitro-based SSDs, with AWS-controlled firmware, cut I/O latency by 60% and jitter by over four times, enhancing reliability and enabling live firmware updates.

The system's architecture has fueled innovation, supporting over 500 instance types, from 1 to 448 vCPUs, and diverse workloads, including Apple M1 and Graviton processors. Brian highlighted the Xen emulation layer, introduced in 2022, which seamlessly migrates legacy Xen-based instances to Nitro, extending their lifespan without customer intervention.

Future-Proofing Cloud Security

The Nitro System positions AWS as a leader in confidential computing, offering built-in security without requiring application modifications. Brian underscored AWS's commitment to continuous innovation, with Nitro underpinning all AWS services. This ensures that customers inherit its security and performance benefits across the platform. The system's isolated network and hot-patching capabilities further enhance reliability, allowing firmware updates without downtime.

For organizations seeking secure, high-performance cloud solutions, the Nitro System sets a new standard, aligning with AWS's mission to prioritize security as a foundational element.

Links:

- AWS Summit Ottawa 2022 Video:

https://www.youtube.com/watch?v=S3x3TXNqJhg
- AWS Skill Builder: https://aws.amazon.com/training/

Hashtags: #AWSSummit #NitroSystem #CloudSecurity #EC2 #CloudComputing #AWS #AmazonWebServices #BrianMycroft

---

Innovation and Data Analytics Solving Real-World Challenges

At the AWS Summit Ottawa 2022, Marianne Schroeder from the University of British Columbia (UBC) and Archer, a Solutions Architect at Amazon Web Services (AWS), delivered a 49-minute session showcasing the UBC Cloud Innovation Centre (CIC). The session highlighted how UBC students leverage machine learning (ML), high-performance computing (HPC), and data analytics to develop open-source prototypes addressing public sector challenges. From predicting heart failure outcomes to optimizing MRI requisitions, the CIC's projects demonstrate the power of cloud technology in solving real-world problems. Below, we explore the session's key themes, enriched with insights from the lecture and AWS's commitment to fostering innovation.

The UBC Cloud Innovation Centre: A Collaborative Hub

Marianne introduced the UBC CIC, a public-private partnership launched in January 2020, born from a 2018 discussion on enhancing education through technology. The CIC collaborates with AWS, which provides three full-time staff and cloud credits, while UBC contributes staff and space. The centre hires students, including 25% from arts disciplines, through co-op programs to work on community health and wellbeing challenges. These students, often with no prior cloud experience, undergo a ramp-up program to build sophisticated prototypes, published under open-source licenses like MIT or Apache.

Archer emphasized the real-world learning environment, where students tackle unbalanced datasets and privacy constraints, unlike the sanitized datasets used in academia. The CIC's mission is to foster innovation by creating one-click deployment prototypes, enabling community members to adopt and extend solutions. This approach has led to 26 completed projects since 2020, despite the pandemic's challenges.

Healthcare Innovations: Heart Failure and MRI Optimization

The session showcased two healthcare projects. The first, in collaboration with Vancouver Coastal Health and Providence Healthcare, aimed to predict heart failure outcomes using ML. Cardiologists provided two years of manually collected data (2018–2020) on comorbidities, medications, and hospitalizations. Archer initially hesitated due to the data's inconsistencies, but students derived synthetic fields, achieving a 70% accurate ML model. This prototype demonstrated feasibility, prompting discussions on automated data collection to save lives.

The second project addressed inefficiencies in MRI requisition processes for Vancouver Coastal Health. The Central Intake Office managed 10,000 requisitions across 11 sites, relying on manual faxed forms. Radiologists' prioritization decisions often led to delays if requisitions were sent to sites with long waitlists. Using Amazon Comprehend Medical and PostgreSQL's natural language processing, students built a system to extract body parts and medical terms from forms, incorporating spell-checkers and word-weighting rules. A user interface allowed radiologists to adjust prioritization rules, standardizing processes and reducing delays. The solution, now in clinical trials, exemplifies practical innovation without relying on AI hype.

Environmental and Global Health Solutions

The CIC's work extended to environmental and global health challenges. The Sea Around Us project, supporting marine ecosystem research, faced website crashes from complex data queries. Using the Amazon Working Backwards process, the team migrated data to Amazon S3, used AWS Glue to extract schemas, and employed Athena for serverless SQL queries. The resulting Jupyter Notebooks, hosted on CloudFront, reduced data requests by 80%, empowering researchers with accessible visualizations. The data is now available on AWS Open Data, enhancing global access.

The Serratus project, an open-science initiative, analyzed 20 million gigabytes of gene sequences to identify RNA viruses, discovering tenfold more viruses than in 130 years of virology research. Using S3 for efficient data processing, the team achieved cost-effective, high-speed genomic sequencing, published in *Nature*. The TapGives project, supporting a Kenyan water filtration charity, developed a USSD-based subscription system to ensure sustainable access to clean water, incorporating local context through a Nairobi-born student.

Democratizing AI: COVID-19 Diagnostics

The CIC's COVID-19 CT diagnostics project, started in January 2020, developed an open-source AI model to assist radiologists. Using 3,000+ CT scans from global sources, the team faced challenges with varying scan quality and de-identification needs. UBC medical students and radiologists annotated lung volumes and opacity patterns, a complex process requiring specialized 3D tools. The resulting ResNet model, now in clinical trials, is accessible via a cost-efficient UI that processes scans on-demand using GPU machines. This democratization of AI highlights the CIC's commitment to impactful, scalable solutions.

Links:

- AWS Summit Ottawa 2022 Video: https://www.youtube.com/watch?v=ZyWyVIsGmBk
- UBC Cloud Innovation Centre: https://cic.ubc.ca/
- AWS Open Data: https://registry.opendata.aws/

Hashtags: #AWSSummit #CloudInnovation #DataAnalytics #MachineLearning #PublicSector #AWS #AmazonWebServices #UBC #Healthcare #OpenSource

Security and Compliance for Container-Based Microservices

In a 47-minute session at AWS Summit Ottawa 2022, Max Neuvians, Head of Site Reliability Engineering at the Canadian Digital Service (CDS), and Nirmal Mehta, AWS Principal Specialist Solutions Architect, explored security and compliance best practices for container-based microservices. With government organizations increasingly adopting containers to modernize applications, this session provided actionable strategies to enhance security while leveraging AWS's shared responsibility model. The presentation combined real-world insights from CDS with technical guidance on securing container environments, emphasizing the mantra of "reduce, reuse, recycle." Below, we delve into the session's core themes, enriched with context from the lecture and AWS's commitment to secure cloud solutions.

Canadian Digital Service: Containers in Action

Max introduced the CDS, a sector within the Treasury Board Secretariat launched in July 2017 to transform government service delivery. Operating as a distributed organization across 40 Canadian locations, CDS builds accessible, inclusive services through its platform and partnerships units. Key products include GC Notify, which has sent over 50 million notifications since 2019, and the COVID Alert server, which handled 2.5 billion API requests with zero downtime from 2020 to 2022. Both run on containers, leveraging Kubernetes, AWS Lambda, and Fargate for scalability and security.

CDS adopted containers to avoid the complexity of managing virtual machines, relying on AWS's expertise in infrastructure. Containers, lightweight software packages containing code and dependencies, are deployed to serverless Lambda for short transactions, Fargate for managed containers, or Kubernetes for complex microservices. Max emphasized that security encompasses reliability and zero downtime, not just preventing exploits, setting the stage for practical recommendations.

Securing Containers: Best Practices from CDS

Max shared CDS's container security strategies, focusing on

simplicity and consistency. Key recommendations include:

- **Know Your Dependencies**: Scan manifests, set alerts for upgrades, and generate software bills of materials (SBOMs) to track vulnerabilities. Automated tools can block releases with critical issues.
- **Use Multi-Stage Builds**: For the CDS website, a Go binary is built in one stage and copied to a minimal scratch container, reducing the attack surface by eliminating unnecessary system files.
- **Choose Minimal Base Images**: The CDS website uses a 50MB scratch image, compared to larger Debian (440MB) or Alpine (250MB) images for other applications. Tailor base images to application needs.
- **Tag with Git SHA**: Tagging containers with Git commit hashes ensures traceability and enables quick rollbacks if vulnerabilities arise.
- **Automate Builds and Deployments**: Automated pipelines reduce errors, with manual actions limited to code reviews. Infrastructure as code enables rapid environment recreation.
- **Test Before Deployment**: Blue-green or canary deployments validate functionality, minimizing risks from faulty containers.
- **Monitor and Respond**: Tools like Falco monitor system calls, with alerts integrated into Slack for rapid incident response. Blameless postmortems foster learning without fear.

Max highlighted CDS's blameless culture, where incidents like database deletions are organizational failures, not individual faults, fostering a psychologically safe environment.

AWS's Defense-in-Depth Approach

Nirmal expanded on container security using the "onion model" of defense-in-depth, where each layer—data, configuration, code, dependencies, container, and host—requires protection. Containers' shared host environment and non-container-aware traditional tools pose challenges, necessitating tailored strategies. Nirmal's "reduce, reuse, recycle" mantra guided his recommendations:

- **Reduce**: Minimize container size and surface area. Use multi-stage builds and lint Dockerfiles with tools like Hadolint to catch errors (e.g., unspecified Debian versions or invalid ports). Avoid monolithic containers with unnecessary components.
- **Reuse**: Standardize small, vetted base images managed by a central team (e.g., SRE or security). Create language-specific

images for 80% of organizational needs, integrating them into CI/CD pipelines.
- **Recycle**: Treat containers as ephemeral, destroying "dirty" containers (e.g., those accessed via SSH). Use ephemeral containers in Kubernetes 1.23 for debugging.

AWS's Elastic Container Registry (ECR) supports security with tag immutability, encryption, and scanning. Basic scanning uses Clair for OS vulnerabilities, while enhanced scanning, powered by Amazon Inspector, covers programming languages and integrates with Security Hub and EventBridge for alerts.

Runtime and Host Security

Nirmal emphasized runtime security:
- **Secrets Management**: Never store secrets in containers. Use AWS Secrets Manager or Parameter Store to inject secrets at runtime, leveraging IAM roles for service accounts.
- **Resource Limits**: Set container resource limits in Kubernetes to prevent overuse, enhancing reliability and security.
- **Non-Root Execution**: Run containers as non-root users, using AppArmor and seccomp to restrict system calls and file access, reducing kernel exploit risks.
- **Policy Enforcement**: Tools like Open Policy Agent and Kyverno enforce policies, ensuring only approved registries are used. CIS benchmarks validate compliance.

For hosts, Nirmal recommended immutable infrastructure with minimal AMIs, regular rolling upgrades, and AWS Bottlerocket, a purpose-built OS for containers with no shell or SSH. AWS Fargate, a serverless compute option, further isolates hosts, minimizing management overhead. Third-party solutions from AWS partners enhance scanning, runtime policies, and forensics.

Links:

- AWS Summit Ottawa 2022 Video:
  https://www.youtube.com/watch?v=6NeQa_1YXbI
- Canadian Digital Service: https://digital.canada.ca/
- EKS Security Best Practices:
  https://aws.github.io/aws-eks-best-practices/security/docs/
- ECS Security Best Practices:

https://docs.aws.amazon.com/AmazonECS/latest/d
eveloperguide/security-best-practices.html

Hashtags: #AWSSummit #ContainerSecurity #Compliance #Microservices #PublicSector #AWS #AmazonWebServices #CanadianDigitalService #MaxNeuvians #NirmalMehta

Data Warehousing Reinvented for Today's Needs

At the AWS Summit Ottawa 2022, David, a Solutions Architect, and Ahmed Shehata, a Senior Data Warehousing Specialist, delivered a 48-minute session on how Amazon Redshift redefines cloud data warehousing to meet modern demands. As data grows exponentially—more is created hourly now than in an entire year two decades ago—organizations face both opportunities and challenges in deriving actionable insights. This session explored how Redshift's scalability, simplicity, and advanced analytics capabilities empower public sector organizations to deliver better services. Below, we dive into the session's key themes, enriched with insights from the lecture and AWS's commitment to customer-driven innovation.

Amazon Redshift: A Robust Data Warehousing Solution

David introduced Amazon Redshift as the leading cloud data warehouse, used by tens of thousands of customers to derive business insights at scale. Redshift addresses six critical criteria for modern data warehousing: ingesting diverse data anytime, anywhere; offering simplicity by abstracting complexity; scaling seamlessly with demand; providing pay-as-you-go pricing; delivering top price performance; and enabling real-time predictive analytics at petabyte scale. These features enhance operational efficiency, support informed decision-making, and accelerate innovation.

Redshift's evolution reflects AWS's customer-centric approach. Launched in 2012 as the first cloud data warehouse, it introduced Redshift Spectrum in 2017 to query data lakes, RA3 nodes in 2019 for independent compute and storage scaling, and Redshift ML in 2021 for integrated machine learning. Ninety percent of Redshift's features stem from customer feedback, ensuring it meets real-world needs like breaking data silos and integrating with modern data architectures.

Simplifying Analytics and Data Access

Redshift simplifies analytics by automating infrastructure management, allowing users to focus on insights rather than maintenance. It supports standard SQL connections to business intelligence tools like Tableau, Looker, and Amazon QuickSight, and integrates with the Redshift Query Editor V2 for authoring queries and stored procedures. The Redshift Data API enables seamless integration with web applications without managing database connections, while spatial SQL functions support geometric data analysis.

Federated queries allow Redshift to query operational databases (e.g., Amazon RDS, Aurora) in place, joining transactional data with warehouse data without full data copies. Redshift Spectrum extends this capability to exabytes of data in Amazon S3, querying data lakes without impacting cluster performance. Materialized views and auto query rewrites enhance performance by caching results and optimizing queries, reducing read impacts and speeding up dashboards and reports.

Scalability and Cost Efficiency

Ahmed highlighted Redshift's scalability, addressing customer challenges with workload spikes (e.g., during reporting periods or events like Christmas). Introduced in 2019, concurrency scaling automatically provisions transient clusters to handle query spikes, scaling down when demand subsides. Customers can enable this for specific workloads, like reporting, and receive 30 hours of free usage monthly—97% of users leverage this without additional costs.

The RA3 node type, also launched in 2019, separates compute and storage, allowing independent scaling. Available in sizes (xlplus, 4xl, 16xl), RA3 nodes reduce costs by avoiding overprovisioning. Redshift Serverless, announced in 2021 and nearing general availability in Canada by late 2022, simplifies provisioning and scales dynamically, charging only for query runtime. Use cases include self-serve analytics for data science teams, workload separation for reporting, and batch ingestion, reducing costs by eliminating idle cluster time.

Security and Compliance for Public Sector Needs

Security is paramount for Redshift, aligning with public sector requirements. It integrates with AWS Identity and Access Management (IAM) and supports identity providers like Azure AD and Okta, with multifactor authentication. Access control offers column-level and role-based privileges, while AWS CloudTrail logs API calls for auditing. Encryption, managed via AWS Key

Management Service (KMS), secures data in transit and at rest, with Lambda UDFs for tokenization. Redshift complies with standards like the Canadian Center for Cybersecurity (CCCS), PCI, SOC, FedRAMP, and HIPAA, ensuring trust for sensitive workloads.

Links:

- AWS Summit Ottawa 2022 Video:
  https://www.youtube.com/watch?v=1aKtYJdP6-I
- Amazon   Redshift   Overview:
  https://aws.amazon.com/redshift/
- AWS Data Analytics Learning Path:
  https://aws.amazon.com/training/learning-paths/data-analytics/

Hashtags: #AWSSummit #DataWarehousing #AmazonRedshift #Analytics   #PublicSector   #AWS   #AmazonWebServices #CloudComputing

Building Modern Data Architecture and Data Mesh Patterns on AWS

In a 49-minute session at AWS Summit Ottawa 2022, Fabrizio Napolitano, a Senior Analytics Specialist Solutions Architect, explored how organizations can modernize their data strategies using AWS to become data-driven. With many organizations struggling to harness data as an asset, Napolitano introduced modern data architectures and the emerging data mesh pattern. This session detailed how AWS's managed and serverless services, like AWS Glue and AWS Lake Formation, enable scalable, secure, and decentralized data platforms. Below, we unpack the session's core themes, enriched with insights from the lecture and AWS's role in fostering data-driven innovation.

Defining Data-Driven Organizations and Modern Data Strategies

Napolitano began by defining a data-driven organization as one that treats data as a product to drive sustained innovation and deliver actionable insights for enhanced user experiences. Despite high aspirations, few organizations succeed due to challenges in managing vast data sources and ensuring accessibility. A modern data strategy combines people, processes, and technology to address these issues, enabling organizations to catalog, govern, and process data effectively.

AWS supports this strategy with a comprehensive suite of analytics and machine learning services. Amazon S3 serves as a scalable, durable data lake foundation, while AWS Glue automatically catalogs data, and AWS Lake Formation adds governance and security. Amazon Athena provides serverless SQL querying, and services like Amazon EMR and AWS Glue process data at scale. Integration with Amazon QuickSight and SageMaker enables visualization and predictive modeling, creating a feedback loop that drives continuous innovation.

Architectural Patterns: Data Lake and Lake House

The session outlined key architectural patterns, starting with the data lake. Data lakes centralize diverse data (batch or streaming) in

Amazon S3, where crawlers catalog metadata into the AWS Glue Data Catalog. Lake Formation applies governance, granting privileges for services like Athena or third-party tools to query data. This pattern ensures data is findable, accessible, interoperable, and reusable (FAIR principles), supporting business intelligence and machine learning workloads.

The lake house architecture extends the data lake by integrating data warehousing and machine learning. Amazon Redshift, with Redshift Spectrum, allows seamless querying of data lake and warehouse data, joining local cluster data with S3. Redshift ML enables SQL-based model creation, while Redshift Serverless supports unpredictable workloads with pay-as-you-go pricing. Federated queries connect operational databases (e.g., Aurora, RDS), and materialized views enhance performance, making lake house architectures ideal for hybrid analytics needs.

Data Mesh: Decentralized Data Ownership

Napolitano introduced data mesh, a pattern coined by Zhamak Dehghani in 2019, designed to address the limitations of centralized data lakes, which can be slow and complex. Data mesh is built on four principles: domain ownership, data as a product, self-serve infrastructure, and federated governance. Each domain team owns its data and pipelines, treating data as a product with clear contracts and documentation. A federated catalog ensures discoverability across domains.

On AWS, data mesh is implemented using multiple AWS accounts for data domains, with Lake Formation's data sharing enabling secure, in-place access. Producers catalog data in the Glue Data Catalog, and a central governance account manages access privileges. Consumers query data via Athena, QuickSight, or SageMaker without moving it, preserving producer control. This decentralized approach enhances scalability and autonomy, as demonstrated by customers like Fannie Mae and J.P. Morgan Chase.

AWS Lake Formation and Federated Queries for Scalability

AWS Lake Formation simplifies data lake security by managing privileges at database, table, or column levels, using a database-like grant model. Tag-based access control streamlines permissions for large user bases, associating tags (e.g., PII, non-PII) with resources and users. This is critical for data mesh, where producers share data products securely across accounts. Lake Formation's integration with the Glue Data Catalog ensures a unified metadata layer.

Athena's federated queries further enhance flexibility, allowing queries across on-premises databases (e.g., Cassandra), AWS services (e.g., DynamoDB), and other clouds (e.g., Azure Synapse, BigQuery). Connectors push query execution to source systems, returning filtered datasets to Athena for joining with data lake data. This capability supports hybrid environments, enabling organizations to unify disparate data sources without extensive ETL processes.

Links:

- AWS Summit Ottawa 2022 Video:
  https://www.youtube.com/watch?v=wdidpZBKryQ
- AWS Lake Formation Overview:
  https://aws.amazon.com/lake-formation/
- AWS Data Analytics Learning Path:
  https://aws.amazon.com/training/learning-paths
  /data-analytics/

Hashtags: #AWSSummit #DataArchitecture #DataMesh #Analytics #PublicSector #AWS #AmazonWebServices #CloudComputing #FabrizioNapolitano

Designing Secure Protection Environments with Veeam and AWS

At the AWS Summit Ottawa 2022, Alex Crandall from Veeam Government Solutions delivered a 28-minute session on building secure data protection environments using Veeam and AWS. With ransomware attacks becoming inevitable—striking organizations at an alarming rate—this session emphasized strategies to safeguard AWS workloads, maintain compliance, and ensure rapid recovery. Crandall highlighted best practices like role segmentation, immutable storage, and automated backup testing to protect against malicious actors, even if admin credentials are compromised. Below, we explore the session's key insights, enriched with AWS and Veeam's collaborative approach to data security.

The Growing Threat of Ransomware and Data Protection Challenges

Crandall opened by underscoring the pervasive threat of ransomware, noting that it's no longer a question of *if* but *when* an organization will be targeted. Citing a 2022 report, he revealed that the average ransomware payment has surged 4.8 times since 2021, nearing $800,000. However, organizations with robust backups recover 75% of their data, highlighting the critical role of preparedness. Malicious actors exploit vulnerabilities like misconfigured edge devices, phishing emails, or human error, needing only one entry point to cause havoc.

Sysadmins face immense pressure to maintain patched systems, monitor alerts, and secure environments. Common pitfalls include missing critical alerts (e.g., unauthorized file access), outdated patches, poor password policies, and lack of network segmentation. Unverified backups and slow restore times further exacerbate risks, rendering backups useless if untested or inaccessible during a crisis. Veeam and AWS address these challenges by combining automation, immutable storage, and role-based access to create resilient protection environments.

Best Practices for Secure Data Protection

Crandall outlined actionable best practices to enhance data security across data centers, public clouds, and SaaS environments.

The cornerstone is Veeam's **3-2-1-1-0 rule**: maintain three data copies on two different media types, with one offsite, one immutable or air-gapped, and zero errors through verified backups. AWS's S3 Object Lock supports immutability, allowing data to be locked for periods (e.g., 7 to 90 days) to prevent tampering, even by compromised accounts.

Network segmentation is vital, separating production, management, and backup environments to limit lateral movement by attackers. AWS's multi-account strategy isolates production and protection subscriptions, ensuring compromised production accounts cannot access backups. Least-privilege access, enforced via AWS Identity and Access Management (IAM) and role-based access control (RBAC), restricts permissions to the minimum required, reducing risks from over-privileged accounts. Multifactor authentication (MFA) and integration with third-party identity providers (e.g., SAML 2.0) further bolster security.

Veeam's Integration with AWS for Robust Protection

Veeam leverages AWS's native APIs to deliver platform-native backups, eliminating the need for agent-based deployments. For example, Veeam triggers EBS snapshots for EC2 instances, processes them to S3, and transitions data to cost-effective tiers like S3 Glacier or Deep Archive, all protected by Object Lock. This approach supports workloads like RDS, EFS, EKS, ECS, and VPC configurations, ensuring comprehensive protection. AWS services like Snowball and Storage Gateway facilitate rapid offsite data transfers, while AWS Key Management Service (KMS) secures data encryption.

Veeam's **SureBackup** and **SureReplica** technologies automate backup testing in isolated environments, verifying recoverability for SQL databases, Active Directory, or custom workloads. Secure Restore scans backups for malware using existing XDR solutions, allowing manual remediation in isolated environments. Instant Recovery mounts backups in under a minute, minimizing downtime, while DataLabs provides SLA validation and dynamic documentation for audit compliance. These features ensure organizations meet recovery time objectives (RTOs) and recovery point objectives (RPOs).

Recovery and Mobility Across Environments

Effective recovery is as critical as prevention. Veeam enables item-level recovery (e.g., specific files or volumes) and full workload restoration to original or new locations, supporting cloud mobility. For instance, backups from on-premises data centers can be restored as native EC2 instances, accelerating cloud migration. Veeam also protects SaaS platforms like Microsoft 365 and plans to support Salesforce backups by late 2022, addressing diverse workloads.

Orchestration ensures workloads are restored in the correct order, with dynamic documentation tracking RTOs, RPOs, and verification steps. For example, a customer restored a misconfigured VPC by comparing backups, resolving communication issues within minutes. Integration with AWS Outposts extends protection to hybrid environments, allowing data to move seamlessly between on-premises and cloud storage.

Links:

- AWS Summit Ottawa 2022 Video:
  https://www.youtube.com/watch?v=yNmVolxzKYo
- Veeam on AWS:
  https://www.veeam.com/aws-backup.html
- AWS Security Learning Path:
  https://aws.amazon.com/training/learning-paths/security/

Hashtags: #AWSSummit #DataProtection #Ransomware #Veeam #AWS #AmazonWebServices #CloudComputing #Security

Creating Accessible Citizen Services with Digital ID Systems

In a 44-minute session at AWS Summit Ottawa 2022, Louis Caron, a Senior Solutions Architect based in Montreal, explored how digital identity systems enable governments to deliver accessible, secure citizen services. As the COVID-19 pandemic accelerated digital transformation, governments worldwide faced the challenge of verifying identities online. Cloud-based digital ID systems offer the speed, scale, and security needed to streamline services like healthcare, voting, and banking. This session examined global approaches, technical models, and AWS's role in deploying these systems. Below, we delve into the session's key themes, enriched with insights from global case studies and AWS's cloud capabilities.

The Evolution and Importance of Digital Identity

Caron traced the history of identity verification, from the single-sheet "passport" of medieval times to the machine-readable passports standardized post-World War I. Today, digital identity extends this concept to cyberspace, where traditional documents like passports or birth certificates are insufficient. Recognized by the United Nations as a fundamental human right, identity enables access to healthcare, education, and voting. However, over one billion people lack legal identity, and two million cannot authenticate digitally, underscoring the urgency of inclusive solutions.

Digital identity uses electronic tokens, biometrics (e.g., fingerprints, facial recognition), or contextual data (e.g., location) to verify individuals online. Governments are investing in these systems to enhance accessibility, combat fraud, and drive economic growth. The COVID-19 crisis exposed gaps in digital infrastructure, as seen in rushed medical passport implementations, prompting accelerated investment in foundational digital IDs that support both public and private sector services.

Global Models of Digital Identity Systems

Caron outlined three primary models for digital identity deployment: centralized, federated, and decentralized. **Centralized systems**, like India's Aadhaar or Argentina's DNI, use a single database with unique identifiers. Aadhaar, launched in 2009, enrolled one billion citizens in six years, incorporating biometrics for scalability. India's open-source MOSIP platform, adopted by countries like the Philippines and Ethiopia, enables customizable deployments.

Federated systems, used by Nordic countries like Sweden and Finland, involve public-private collaboration. Since 2014, these nations have shared a framework allowing cross-border recognition of digital credentials, enabling a Swedish citizen to use their digital ID in Norway. **Decentralized systems**, pioneered by Estonia since 2001, leverage blockchain to distribute data across multiple locations, enhancing availability. Estonia's "data embassy" concept stores citizen data in foreign data centers while maintaining sovereignty, ensuring service access abroad.

Each model has trade-offs. Centralized systems risk single points of failure, federated systems require cross-entity coordination, and decentralized systems demand advanced technology like blockchain. Governments must align their choice with cultural values, legal frameworks, and technical capabilities.

Challenges and Considerations for Deployment

Deploying digital identity systems is not solely a technical endeavor; it involves significant social, legal, and governance challenges. Social acceptability is critical, as citizens demand transparency and control over their data. Self-sovereign identity, as practiced in Estonia, empowers citizens to authorize data sharing (e.g., with banks) without exposing sensitive details, enhancing trust.

Legal hurdles can derail projects. Kenya's NIIMS system, launched without adequate privacy protections, was declared illegal in 2021, forcing a redesign. Similarly, early faxed signatures lacked legal recognition, illustrating how laws lag behind technology. Interoperability is another challenge, requiring global frameworks to ensure digital IDs are recognized across borders, as seen in the EU's 2020 agreement on data models.

Governance questions—who owns the data, how is consent managed, and who maintains the system—are pivotal. Canada's Digital Identity and Authentication Council (DIAC) addresses this through the Pan-Canadian Trust Framework, ensuring provincial systems are interoperable while respecting regional autonomy. The G20's 2021 recognition of digital identity as a priority underscores its global importance.

AWS's Role in Secure, Scalable Digital Identity

AWS provides the infrastructure to deploy digital identity systems with unparalleled security, agility, and scalability. Security is paramount, as systems face over 5,000 unauthorized access attempts per second, per British Columbia's CIO. AWS's tools, like AWS Key Management Service (KMS) and IAM, secure data and access, while automated testing and incident response capabilities mitigate risks. Standards like NIST's Digital Identity Guidelines and ISO's data models align with AWS's frameworks, ensuring compliance.

Cloud agility allows rapid adaptation to evolving technologies, critical for iterative deployments. AWS's global regions and availability zones ensure 24/7 reliability, vital for citizen-facing services. Scalability supports proof-of-concept testing for millions of users—essential for countries like Canada or India—and handles unpredictable transaction volumes post-launch. Cost-effective pricing models, such as AWS's savings plans, optimize expenses for long-term deployments.

Links:

- AWS Summit Ottawa 2022 Video:
  https://www.youtube.com/watch?v=CWpGVx4iECU
- AWS Institute Digital Identity Guide:
  https://aws.amazon.com/institute/
- AWS Public Sector Learning Path:
  https://aws.amazon.com/training/learning-paths/public-sector/

Hashtags: #AWSSummit #DigitalIdentity #CitizenServices #AWS #AmazonWebServices #CloudComputing #PublicSector

Journey to Protected Workloads on AWS

At the AWS Summit Ottawa 2022, James Kierstead, a Solutions Architect based in Ottawa, delivered a 48-minute session titled "Journey to Protected Workloads on AWS." Focused on public sector customers, particularly the Federal Government of Canada, the session detailed the rigorous process of achieving an Authority to Operate (ATO) through the Security Assessment and Authorization (SA&A) process. Kierstead highlighted AWS's investments in tools like the Secure Environment Accelerator and AWS Audit Manager to streamline compliance, reduce manual effort, and accelerate application deployment. This post explores the session's key insights, enriched with AWS's compliance strategies and practical resources.

Understanding the Security Assessment and Authorization Process

The SA&A process, often referred to as SCNA in Canada, is a critical step for public sector organizations to ensure applications meet security frameworks like the Canadian Centre for Cyber Security's (CCCS) Cloud Medium profile (formerly PBMM). Kierstead explained that this process involves implementing security controls, compiling evidence (e.g., screenshots, API responses), and navigating reviews by external assessors. The goal is to secure an ATO from a Chief Security Officer, which can take months due to manual evidence collection and iterative reviews.

A 2022 AWS survey revealed that 80% of organizations lack automated compliance processes, with governance teams spending over 60% of their time collecting evidence manually. AWS addresses this through its **shared responsibility model**, where AWS secures the cloud infrastructure (hardware, software, facilities), while customers handle security *in* the cloud (e.g., application configurations, encryption). By leveraging AWS's compliance certifications—like PCI-DSS, HIPAA, FedRAMP, and CCCS Cloud Medium—customers inherit robust controls, reducing their compliance burden.

AWS Tools for Streamlining Compliance

AWS offers several tools to simplify the SA&A process. The **AWS**

Secure Environment Accelerator, an open-source solution available on GitHub, automates the implementation of 70% of CCCS Cloud Medium technical controls. By defining a configuration file, customers can deploy these controls in days, compared to months of manual effort. Over 45 public sector customers have adopted this accelerator, significantly reducing setup time.

Additionally, AWS collaborated with the Canadian Border Services Agency (CBSA) to create a **generic evidence package**, which provides evidence for 91 technical controls. This package, sanitized for reuse, serves as a starting point for customers to customize with their environment-specific outputs. Available through AWS account teams, it has been used by 24 customers to accelerate evidence compilation, though assessors' interpretations may vary.

The **AWS Artifact console** provides access to compliance reports, including the CCCS assessment summary for the AWS Canada region. Customers can download these reports to verify service compliance, with detailed reports available through direct requests to CCCS. These resources help customers align their applications with regulatory requirements efficiently.

Automating Evidence Collection with AWS Audit Manager

A standout feature of the session was the introduction of **AWS Audit Manager**, a cloud-native tool designed to automate evidence collection and simplify compliance assessments. Audit Manager continuously evaluates AWS resource usage, mapping it to frameworks like CCCS Cloud Medium, PCI-DSS, and CIS. It collects evidence from sources like AWS Config, CloudTrail, and Security Hub, storing it in an immutable evidence store for two years.

Kierstead demonstrated how Audit Manager generates assessment reports, including PDF summaries and evidence folders, which can be exported to S3. The tool supports multi-account environments through AWS Organizations, consolidating evidence into a single delegated administrator account. Benefits include:

- **Prebuilt frameworks**: CCCS Cloud Medium includes 165 control sets with 602 controls, 206 of which are fully automated.
- **Custom frameworks**: Customers can tailor controls to specific needs, such as Canada's 12 guardrails for cloud accounts.

- **Time savings**: Automated collection frees teams to focus on reviewing evidence and addressing non-compliance.

For example, Audit Manager can verify EBS encryption compliance by scanning CloudTrail API calls and Config rules, presenting results in a centralized console. This reduces the manual effort of checking multiple sources, making reassessments easier when application architectures change.

Practical Steps for Achieving an ATO

Kierstead emphasized the importance of early assessor engagement to clarify control requirements and avoid rework. Customers can inherit controls from AWS's CCCS region assessment or accelerators like the Secure Environment Accelerator, which may already have an ATO. This "stacked assessment" approach allows application teams to focus on app-specific controls, accelerating the SA&A process.

Links:

- AWS Summit Ottawa 2022 Video:
  https://www.youtube.com/watch?v=j_cdj5X_jDo
- AWS Artifact: https://aws.amazon.com/artifact/
- AWS Security Learning Path:
  https://aws.amazon.com/training/learning-paths/security/

Hashtags: #AWSSummit #Security #Compliance #PublicSector #AWS #AmazonWebServices #CloudComputing

AWS Secure Hybrid Edge Services with AWS Outposts

The AWS Summit Ottawa 2022 featured a 49-minute session on AWS secure hybrid edge services, presented by Edgar Valderrama and Tareq, a Solutions Architect based in Montreal. The session explored how AWS Outposts, Local Zones, and Snow Family devices enable organizations to address low latency, data residency, and local data processing needs. With a focus on public sector and enterprise use cases, the presenters highlighted how hybrid solutions accelerate digital transformation and support disaster recovery. This post delves into the session's key insights, enriched with real-world examples like Netflix and technical details on Outposts.

Overview of AWS Hybrid Edge Services

AWS hybrid edge services bridge on-premises and cloud environments, addressing challenges like data residency, low latency, and local processing. Valderrama outlined four key offerings:

- **AWS Outposts**: Fully managed racks or servers deployed in customer data centers, running AWS services like EC2, EBS, S3, RDS, and EKS. Outposts connect to an AWS region via a service link, ideal for low-latency applications and data residency compliance.
- **Local Zones**: Managed infrastructure in metro areas (e.g., Vancouver, Toronto) offering low-latency access to a subset of AWS services (12 services, compared to 200+ in regions).
- **Wavelength**: Compute and storage solutions integrated with telco 5G networks for ultra-low-latency applications like gaming and stock trading.
- **Snow Family**: Devices like Snowball Edge and Snowcone for edge computing and storage, supporting offline scenarios (e.g., naval ships, ambulances) with EC2, S3, and AI capabilities.

These services enable organizations to comply with regulations, reduce costs, and enhance performance. For example, Netflix deployed Local Zones in Los Angeles to provide low-latency remote desktops, boosting employee productivity.

Deep Dive into AWS Outposts

Tareq provided a technical overview of AWS Outposts, describing them as a "logical construct" that extends AWS infrastructure to on-premises data centers. Outposts are fully managed, with AWS handling hardware patching and software updates, while customers manage physical security, power, cooling, and network connectivity. Key features include:

- **Hardware**: Industry-standard 42U racks or 1U/2U servers, some with Graviton processors for high performance. Racks support up to 240 terabytes of S3 storage and 55 terabytes of EBS per host.
- **Services**: Support for EC2, EBS, S3, RDS (SQL Server, PostgreSQL), EKS, ECS, EMR, and VMware Cloud. Local snapshots and backups to S3 are available.
- **Connectivity**: A service link (VPN or Direct Connect) to an AWS region ensures control plane access, though brief network outages (minutes to an hour) are tolerable.

Outposts address three primary use cases: low latency (e.g., gaming), data residency (e.g., public sector compliance), and local data processing (e.g., healthcare imaging). Pricing is transparent, with three-year commitments and options for monthly, partial, or full upfront payments.

Disaster Recovery and Capacity Planning

Outposts support robust disaster recovery strategies, leveraging tools like **CloudEndure** for near real-time EBS replication and **DataSync** for S3 data movement between Outposts or to regions. Customers can replicate data from Outpost to Outpost, Outpost to region, or region to Outpost, ensuring compliance with data residency policies. Tareq emphasized planning for multiple failure scenarios:

- **Network failure**: Redundant routers and links (e.g., Direct Connect with VPN backup) mitigate brief outages.
- **Instance failure**: Auto-scaling groups ensure application resilience.
- **Server failure**: Extra capacity per instance family (e.g., C5, M5) is required, as instances cannot run on different host types.
- **Data center failure**: Multiple Outposts in separate locations, anchored to different availability zones, provide resilience.

Capacity planning is critical, as Outposts lack the elastic scaling of regions. Customers must plan for peak usage, growth, and failures, monitoring utilization via CloudWatch. Valderrama noted that AWS includes 5–15% growth capacity in initial deployments to accommodate future needs.

Real-World Applications and Customer Considerations

The session highlighted practical applications, such as healthcare IoT (processing medical imaging on Outposts) and industrial IoT (edge analytics for manufacturing). The Photobox case study demonstrated how Snowball Edge migrated 10 petabytes of data to the cloud, enabling AI-driven innovation. Public sector customers benefit from Outposts' ability to keep sensitive data on-premises while leveraging AWS services.

Customers must consider the **shared responsibility model**, where AWS secures the cloud, but customers handle physical security, environmental controls, and capacity management. Outposts are not purchased but consumed as a managed service, with AWS retaining ownership. For procurement challenges, AWS collaborates with customers to navigate contractual requirements, as seen with Canadian public sector clients.

Links:

- AWS Summit Ottawa 2022 Video: https://www.youtube.com/watch?v=uBn6TbTVCOQ
- AWS Outposts: https://aws.amazon.com/outposts/
- AWS Public Sector Learning Path: https://aws.amazon.com/training/learning-paths/public-sector/

Hashtags: #AWSSummit #HybridCloud #Outposts #PublicSector #AWS #AmazonWebServices #CloudComputing

Enhancing Customer Engagement with Video Chat

At the AWS Summit Ottawa 2022, Enid Zambrano and Joe Trelli presented a 39-minute session titled "Improve Digital Customer Engagement with Video Chat." The session showcased how integrating Amazon Chime SDK with Amazon Connect enables organizations to embed video channels into contact centers, enhancing customer engagement while maintaining cost efficiency. Through a live demo and technical insights, the presenters highlighted use cases like license renewals and remote proctoring. This post explores the session's key takeaways, enriched with AWS's contact center capabilities and practical implementation strategies.

The Power of Amazon Connect and Chime SDK

Amazon Connect is an omnichannel cloud contact center that supports voice, chat, tasks, and now video through integration with Amazon Chime SDK. Zambrano, an Amazon Connect Specialist with over 25 years of experience, emphasized its ability to deliver personalized, dynamic customer experiences. A 2022 AWS study noted that 85% of customers expect seamless omnichannel interactions, yet 70% of contact centers struggle with legacy systems. Amazon Connect addresses this by offering scalable, pay-as-you-go pricing and native integrations with AWS services.

The **Amazon Chime SDK**, as Trelli explained, is a builder-focused software development kit for embedding real-time voice, video, and messaging into applications. It powers use cases like Slack's "huddles" feature and MindBody's virtual fitness classes, supporting up to 250 participants. With 18 global media regions, it minimizes latency, ensuring high-quality interactions. The SDK's WebRTC-based video, SIP trunking, and elastic messaging channels (up to 1 million users) make it versatile for contact centers and beyond.

Live Demo: Streamlining License Renewals

The session featured a demo illustrating a customer (Joe) renewing a driver's license online without visiting an office. The customer interacts via a website embedded with Amazon Connect's chat, authenticating their identity and entering a queue. The agent (Enid), using a unified desktop, accesses Joe's details, initiates a video call via Chime SDK, and verifies his identity by comparing his live feed to a stored photo. The demo showcased:

- **Omnichannel flexibility**: Agents handle chat, voice, and video simultaneously, with historical context preserved.
- **Personalization**: Preloaded customer data enables tailored greetings, like "Hello Joe, I see you're renewing your license."
- **Scheduling**: Video calls can be scheduled for later, ensuring flexibility for customers.
- **Security**: Integration with Amazon Rekognition supports facial recognition, addressing concerns like deep fakes.

The demo highlighted how Amazon Connect's Contact Control Panel (CCP) unifies interactions, while Chime SDK delivers seamless video, reducing operational costs by 20% for similar implementations, per AWS customer data.

Technical Architecture and Integration

For technical audiences, Zambrano and Trelli detailed the architecture behind the demo. The process begins with a customer engaging via a website or app, triggering Amazon Connect's contact flows to route them to the appropriate agent based on skill-based routing. When video is required, Amazon Connect communicates with Chime SDK via **AWS Lambda**, a serverless service that orchestrates the video session. Key components include:

- **Amazon Connect**: Manages queues, routing, and agent desktops, with integrations like Contact Lens for sentiment analysis and Wisdom for real-time knowledge retrieval.
- **Amazon Chime SDK**: Provides WebRTC-based video, audio, and content sharing, with pay-as-you-go pricing (e.g., $0.0017 per minute for video).
- **AWS Lambda**: Facilitates communication between Connect and Chime SDK, ensuring seamless session initiation.
- **Supporting services**: Amazon Lex for chatbots, Voice ID for voice authentication, and Rekognition for facial analysis enhance security and automation.

This architecture supports remote agents, requiring only an internet connection and headset, and scales dynamically to handle peak loads. The session noted that 60% of AWS customers report faster deployment times with Connect compared to legacy systems.

Broader Use Cases and Implementation Tips

Beyond license renewals, Chime SDK and Connect support diverse use cases, such as:

- **Remote proctoring**: Universities use video to monitor exams securely.
- **Telehealth**: Doctors conduct virtual consultations with screen pops for medical data.
- **Financial services**: Banks verify identities for high-value transactions.

To implement, Zambrano recommended starting with AWS's **Working Backwards workshops** to align solutions with business needs. AWS Skill Builder offers training on Connect and Chime SDK, while immersion days provide hands-on experience. For authentication, combining Voice ID, Rekognition, and custom code (e.g., one-time codes via Chime SDK) mitigates deep fake risks. Customers should leverage **Amazon Connect Canada** (Canada Central 1) for compliance with local data residency requirements.

Links:

- AWS Summit Ottawa 2022 Video:
  https://www.youtube.com/watch?v=Of4vHv40cYQ
- Amazon Connect: https://aws.amazon.com/connect/
- Amazon Chime SDK:
  https://aws.amazon.com/chime/chime-sdk/

Hashtags: #AWSSummit #ContactCenter #VideoChat #PublicSector #AWS #AmazonWebServices #CloudComputing

Replatforming to Amazon EKS for Enhanced Reliability

The AWS Summit Ottawa 2022 featured a 42-minute session titled "Replatform to Amazon EKS," presented by Ryan Jaeger and Jonathan Oliver. Jaeger, a Solutions Architect, introduced Amazon Elastic Kubernetes Service (EKS), while Oliver, from LandSure Systems, shared their cloud journey, detailing how EKS improved reliability and availability for British Columbia's land title systems. The session emphasized multi-account strategies and multi-tenant EKS clusters, offering practical insights for public sector customers. This post explores the session's key lessons, enriched with AWS's Kubernetes capabilities and LandSure's transformation.

Understanding Amazon EKS and Its Benefits

Amazon EKS simplifies the deployment and management of containerized applications at scale, addressing the complexities of self-managed Kubernetes. Jaeger highlighted that 75% of organizations struggle with Kubernetes management, spending 60% of operational time on upgrades and monitoring. EKS, a fully upstream, certified Kubernetes distribution, mitigates this through:

- **Managed control plane**: AWS handles API servers, persistence layers, and patching across multiple availability zones, ensuring high availability.
- **Integration with AWS services**: EKS supports Elastic Load Balancing, IAM, VPC, and CloudTrail for scalability and security.
- **Long-term support**: Up to four Kubernetes versions are supported, with backported patches, allowing phased upgrades.
- **Simplified operations**: EKS reduces complexity, enabling teams to focus on applications rather than infrastructure.

By offloading "undifferentiated heavy lifting," EKS frees organizations to innovate, as LandSure's case demonstrated.

LandSure's Cloud Journey: From On-Prem to EKS

LandSure Systems, a subsidiary of British Columbia's Land Title and Survey Authority (LTSA), manages mission-critical systems for land title and survey records. Oliver described their transition from a traditional three-tier architecture (web, application, database servers) to containerization. Initially, LandSure adopted OKD (upstream OpenShift) on-premises, but faced challenges:

- **Operational overhead**: Managing clusters consumed significant resources, with issues like unreliable persistent volume claims and Helm failures.
- **Scalability limitations**: Adding nodes required rebuilding clusters, disrupting operations.
- **Aging infrastructure**: Servers, treated as "pets," were outdated, hindering modernization.

Four years ago, LandSure embraced AWS, replatforming to EKS. Using **infrastructure as code** (Ansible, Terraform, Helm), they containerized Java applications, achieving 100% uptime in the first four months compared to 98% on-premises. EKS resolved ingress, Helm, and storage issues, with Amazon Elastic File System (EFS) enabling shared file systems for legacy apps.

Building a Multi-Tenant EKS Cluster

LandSure faced "cluster sprawl" with over 12 EKS clusters across 30 accounts, complicating deployments. To address this, they consolidated into a multi-tenant EKS architecture, reducing clusters to two (non-prod and prod). Oliver outlined the approach:

- **Shared accounts**: A networking account centralized VPCs, transit gateways, and NAT gateways, while a security account integrated a Fortinet firewall for traffic inspection.
- **Platform team account**: Managed EKS clusters, CI/CD runners, and Helm, with segregated node groups for tenants.
- **Consumer accounts**: Product teams deployed workloads in tenant namespaces, restricted to their sandbox to prevent cluster-wide actions.
- **IAM Roles for Service Accounts (IRSA)**: Enabled cross-account access, allowing workloads in the platform account to interact with resources (e.g., S3, DynamoDB) in consumer accounts securely.

Hierarchical Namespaces (HNS), a Kubernetes feature, allowed tenants to create sub-namespaces without platform team intervention, enhancing autonomy. This consolidation cut operational costs by 20% and simplified deployments from days to two hours.

Practical Tips for EKS Adoption

The session offered actionable advice for organizations adopting EKS:

- **Start with a landing zone**: Design a multi-account structure with management, security, networking, and workload accounts to ensure isolation and cost tracking.
- **Leverage infrastructure as code**: Tools like Terraform and Ansible streamline provisioning and ensure consistency.
- **Use managed services**: EKS's managed node groups and auto-scaling simplify scaling, as LandSure's node addition experience showed.
- **Train teams**: AWS Skill Builder offers EKS courses, while workshops like AWS Immersion Days provide hands-on learning.
- **Engage AWS support**: Solutions architects can guide multi-tenant designs and compliance, especially for public sector clients.

LandSure's success underscores the importance of avoiding self-managed Kubernetes pitfalls and embracing AWS's managed services.

Links:

- AWS Summit Ottawa 2022 Video:
  https://www.youtube.com/watch?v=3V1Yxsry9GA
- Amazon EKS: https://aws.amazon.com/eks/
- AWS Public Sector Learning Path:
  https://aws.amazon.com/training/learning-paths/public-sector/

Hashtags: #AWSSummit #Kubernetes #EKS #PublicSector #AWS #AmazonWebServices #CloudComputing

Digital Training for Canada's Government Workforce

At the AWS Summit Ottawa 2022, a 45-minute panel titled "Digital Training for the Government Workforce" explored how the Canada School of Public Service (CSPS) and D2L, leveraging Amazon Web Services (AWS), transformed learning for 300,000 public servants. Moderated by Fahd Gulzar, the panel featured Taki Sarantakis, CSPS President, and Nick Oddson, D2L's Chief Technology Officer. The session highlighted the implementation of D2L's Brightspace Learning Management System (LMS), addressing the cloud skills gap and modernizing government training. This post delves into the session's insights, the cultural shift required, and the benefits of cloud-based learning.

Brightspace: A Cloud-Powered Learning Revolution

In February 2022, CSPS deployed Brightspace, a cloud-native LMS by D2L, across the Government of Canada, serving 300,000 employees in all provinces, territories, and abroad. Sarantakis noted that 250,000 users had already signed up, with 10,000 accessing it daily. Built entirely on AWS, Brightspace offers near-perfect reliability—down for a maximum of three hours in six months, compared to frequent outages in the prior 2014 system. AWS's scalability eliminates traditional scaling concerns, enabling seamless access akin to global platforms like Netflix or Google.

Brightspace's intuitive interface requires no training, aligning with modern user expectations for simplicity, as seen in consumer platforms like Amazon or Google. This accessibility supports bilingual delivery and global reach, critical for public servants in diverse roles, from Global Affairs to Immigration. The platform's cloud architecture, leveraging AWS's infrastructure as code, ensures agility, allowing rapid configuration without code modifications, reducing deployment risks.

Overcoming Cultural and Technical Barriers

Implementing Brightspace required significant cultural and technical shifts. Sarantakis highlighted the government's historical reluctance to innovate due to risk aversion, preferring proven technologies to avoid failures like the U.S. Obamacare portal launch. However, rapid technological advancements necessitate modern tools like cloud, SaaS, and AI to meet citizen expectations for instant, reliable services. CSPS's prior system, despite being "modern" by government standards, was cumbersome, requiring weeks for updates and frequent maintenance.

The biggest challenge was internal resistance. Sarantakis's team initially viewed their system as adequate, citing familiarity and data integration. Convincing them to aim for an "amazing" platform required a mindset shift, emphasizing user experience over complacency. On the technical side, this was the Government of Canada's first nationwide SaaS and cloud contract, necessitating new approaches to security, accessibility, and procurement, traditionally designed for on-premises systems. D2L and CSPS collaborated closely, conducting gap analyses and iterative testing from March 2021 to the Valentine's Day 2022 launch, ensuring compliance with Protected B workloads and advanced cryptography.

Benefits for Learners and Instructors

Brightspace's deployment has transformed learning for public servants and instructors. For learners, the platform offers engaging, accessible content, supporting lifelong learning critical in 2022's fast-evolving landscape. Sarantakis emphasized that learning is no longer confined to youth; adults must continuously upskill to remain relevant. Brightspace's intuitive design, informed by D2L's universal design principles, ensures accessibility for all, including those with visual or mobility challenges, aligning with Canada's goal to be a global accessibility leader.

Instructors and course designers benefit from self-service capabilities, eliminating reliance on IT intermediaries. Previously, 30–40 tech staff handled content updates, slowing delivery. Now, instructors work natively within Brightspace, focusing on teaching and design. This efficiency mirrors AWS's "core competence" principle, allowing CSPS to prioritize mission-critical tasks. The platform's agility enables real-time content updates, ensuring evergreen material—vital when outdated references, like mentioning a past prime minister, needed quick correction.

Paving the Way for Future Innovation

The CSPS-D2L partnership sets a precedent for government modernization. As the first government-wide cloud and SaaS initiative, it navigated uncharted territory, establishing frameworks for security, accessibility, and procurement that future departments, like Transport Canada or Service Canada, can leverage. Other agencies are already adopting Brightspace for specialized training, such as food or railway inspection, via multi-tenancy agreements, reducing setup time and costs.

For D2L, this project opens opportunities to serve other government agencies, building on Brightspace's scalability and AWS's reliability. Oddson noted that the cloud's ability to handle peak loads—evident during back-to-school surges—ensures performance under pressure. The collaboration's success, driven by a partnership mindset rather than a vendor-buyer dynamic, demonstrates that such transformations are achievable. Sarantakis hopes this becomes "boring" and routine, signaling widespread government adoption of modern platforms.

Links:

- AWS Summit Ottawa 2022 Video:
  https://www.youtube.com/watch?v=cK_FUqPfHaU
- D2L Brightspace: https://www.d2l.com/brightspace/
- Canada School of Public Service:
  https://www.csps-efpc.gc.ca/

Hashtags: #AWSSummit #DigitalTraining #PublicSector #AWS #CloudComputing #GovernmentInnovation #LifelongLearning

Driving Change with Amazon's Culture of Innovation

The AWS Summit Ottawa 2022 featured a 49-minute session titled "Drive Change with Amazon's Culture of Innovation," presented by an Amazon speaker and Michael Tromblay, President and CEO of Invest Ottawa. The session explored Amazon's customer-centric innovation framework and how Invest Ottawa applies similar principles to foster economic growth. Emphasizing mechanisms like the Working Backwards process and cultural pillars, the session offered actionable insights for public sector organizations. This post unpacks Amazon's innovation strategies and Invest Ottawa's regional impact, enriched with AWS's broader context.

Amazon's Customer-Centric Innovation Framework

Amazon's innovation begins with its mission to be "Earth's most customer-centric company," a deliberate focus driving diverse businesses, from e-commerce to AWS's 200+ services. The speaker highlighted the 2016 shareholder letter by Jeff Bezos, noting customers' perpetual dissatisfaction fuels innovation, even when they're satisfied. This mindset applies universally—citizens, patients, or students seek better experiences, relevant to public sector missions.

The **growth flywheel** underpins Amazon's strategy: offering vast selection, low prices, and convenience enhances customer experience, driving traffic and attracting third-party sellers or partners, increasing selection. Economies of scale reduce costs, enabling lower prices, further improving experience. In the public sector, this translates to digital services reducing pressure on legacy systems, as seen in the UK Passport Office's digital transformation, freeing resources for innovation. The speaker challenged attendees to define their organization's flywheel.

Cultural and Mechanistic Pillars of Innovation

Amazon's innovation rests on four pillars: culture, mechanisms, architecture, and organization. **Culture** emphasizes hiring builders with a customer-obsessed mindset, guided by 16 leadership principles like "Invent and Simplify" and "Bias for Action." These principles, sometimes seemingly contradictory (e.g., "Dive Deep" vs. "Bias for Action"), foster innovation by encouraging calculated risks and accepting being misunderstood, as with Kindle's 2007 launch or AWS's 2006 "risky bet," now serving millions monthly.

Mechanisms, like the Working Backwards process, facilitate innovation. This involves drafting a fictional press release and FAQ (PRFAQ) to clarify ideas before execution, focusing on customer pain points and benefits. For example, the AWS Cloud Innovation Center at UBC began with a PRFAQ, leading to initiatives like COVID X-ray analysis. This low-cost, iterative process helps prioritize ideas, applicable to public sector projects needing stakeholder alignment. The speaker encouraged attendees to explore similar mechanisms.

Architectural and Organizational Agility

Amazon's **architecture** shifted from a monolithic to a microservices environment around 2000, enabling parallel development and tens of thousands of daily deployments, compared to weekly updates previously. This agility, foundational to AWS's self-service model, allows builders to experiment quickly and fail inexpensively, accelerating innovation. Public sector organizations can adopt microservices to modernize legacy systems, reducing risks and enhancing scalability, as AWS's 111 price reductions demonstrate.

Organizationally, Amazon uses "two-pizza teams"—small, autonomous groups owning their work, including DevOps responsibilities. This structure avoids committee bloat, fostering nimbleness and accountability. Failures, like the Fire Phone, are celebrated as learning opportunities, with its team later building Amazon Echo. The speaker urged attendees to consider small, empowered teams to drive public sector innovation, balancing risk with rapid experimentation.

Invest Ottawa's Innovation in Action

Michael Tromblay showcased Invest Ottawa's less structured but impactful approach to regional innovation. Operating on Algonquin and Anishinaabe land, Invest Ottawa attracts foreign investment and supports entrepreneurship, leveraging Ottawa's strengths: one in five employees in government, one in nine in tech (North America's highest density), and a rebounding tourism sector. Innovation, Tromblay argued, combines invention with commercialization, citing Ottawa's unicorns like Shopify and billion-dollar ventures like Ascent Compliance.

During the pandemic, Invest Ottawa delivered programs like Digital Main Street, aiding 1,700 businesses with e-commerce solutions, and provided $16 million to 1,400 businesses post-Ottawa occupation. The **SheBoot program**, launched in 2020, supports female founders, raising $11 million for participants. **Area X.O**, a 1,800-acre "future plex," tests autonomous vehicles and smart farming, leveraging advanced communication systems (5G, LoRa). These initiatives, often partnered with AWS, demonstrate practical innovation, aligning with Amazon's customer-focused ethos.

Links:

- AWS Summit Ottawa 2022 Video:
  https://www.youtube.com/watch?v=zsAxk2Uo_wQ
- Invest Ottawa: https://investottawa.ca/
- AWS Leadership Principles:
  https://www.amazon.jobs/en/principles

Hashtags: #AWSSummit #Innovation #PublicSector #AWS #CloudComputing #CustomerCentric #InvestOttawa

Why Digital Government is Essential

At the AWS Summit Ottawa 2022, a 45-minute session titled "Why Digital Government is Essential" underscored the necessity of digital transformation for public sector organizations. Moderated by Ray Hessian, AWS's leader for Canadian national security and defense customers, the panel featured Liam Maxwell, AWS Director of Government Transformation, and Philippa Manly, Director of Projects and Digital Services at Her Majesty's Passport Office (HMPO) in the UK. The session explored how cloud computing enhances innovation, agility, and resilience while reducing costs, using HMPO's digital passport service as a case study. This post delves into the session's key insights, emphasizing trust, user-centric design, and practical transformation strategies.

The Imperative of Digital Transformation

Maxwell opened by emphasizing that digital transformation transcends digitizing data or cloud migration; it requires evolving people, processes, and culture. With citizens expecting seamless digital services, governments face pressure to innovate despite budget and staffing constraints. Cloud computing, Maxwell argued, is pivotal for delivering scalable, secure services. He cited global examples: New South Wales Pathology used AWS Connect to streamline COVID test result delivery, reducing wait times; Rhode Island modernized a 30-year-old COBOL system to handle unemployment claims; and Sardinia's Cagliari region shifted to remote government services in a week using AWS Workspaces. These cases highlight cloud's ability to enable rapid, citizen-focused solutions.

In India, AWS supported the vaccination of 25 million people daily, registering 1.4 billion users, showcasing cloud's scalability. Maxwell outlined four transformation drivers: a bold vision (e.g., UK's Digital by Default), clear benefits (cost savings, agility), executive buy-in, and sustained momentum. These principles, grounded in AWS's global experience, guide governments to prioritize user needs over organizational structures.

Building Trust Through User-Centric Services

A core theme was building citizen trust through services designed around users, not departments. Maxwell noted that legacy systems often mirrored organizational silos, frustrating users. Digital transformation flips this, enabling services tailored to citizen needs. The UK's shift to cloud in 2013, supported by the National Cybersecurity Centre, simplified security classifications, raising the bar for all government data. This reform reduced inter-departmental confusion and enhanced security, allowing faster service delivery.

Maxwell highlighted transparency as a trust enabler. The UK's digital transformation program openly shared successes and failures, empowering civil servants to take risks. Tools like iPads in Downing Street allowed real-time service monitoring, fostering accountability. Globally, AWS's Open Government Solutions webpage curates shareable code and policies, encouraging collaboration among governments. This openness, Maxwell argued, accelerates innovation, as public sectors lack competitive barriers and can leverage shared solutions.

HMPO's Digital Passport Transformation

Philippa Manly provided a practical example with HMPO's digital passport service. HMPO, the sole issuer of UK passports, processes 6–7 million applications annually, alongside civil registration services. In 2014, a demand surge exposed HMPO's paper-based, inefficient processes. Applications required a 26-page guide, specific pens, and error-prone forms, leading to rework and frustrated citizens. A media storm and political scrutiny forced action, coinciding with the UK's Digital by Default initiative.

HMPO's business case focused on citizen expectations for digital, world-class services, better data utilization, and replacing aging IT systems. Starting with a small, multidisciplinary team, HMPO built an online application prototype, testing iteratively to establish scalable patterns. Dual-running legacy and digital systems mitigated risks, while continuous integration enabled frequent updates. Partnerships with external experts built internal capability, ensuring HMPO wasn't vendor-locked. The result: a near-fully digital service where citizens enter tailored data, upload photos via smartphones, and track applications in real-time, integrated with Gov Notify for SMS updates.

Outcomes and Future Directions

HMPO's transformation yielded significant benefits. Over 90% of applicants now use the digital service, reducing paper handling and customer contacts by 90%. Satisfaction scores exceed 90%, earning HMPO awards like the UK Government's Data and Technology Award. Internally, automated checks and decision engines cut examination times by 50%, leveraging clean digital data. During COVID, HMPO maintained operations remotely, handling 9 million applications in 2022 despite fivefold volume spikes in some areas. Features like front-end throttling ensure resilience.

Challenges remain, including eliminating residual paper processes and integrating with civil registration to remove document requirements. HMPO aims to expand its data services, supporting initiatives like single government sign-on. Manly emphasized learning from global peers, inviting attendees to share experiences. The session concluded with Maxwell reinforcing that dual-running and cloud adoption are critical for navigating legacy constraints, offering a model for Canadian agencies like Service Canada or Immigration, Refugees and Citizenship Canada.

Links:

- AWS Summit Ottawa 2022 Video:
  https://www.youtube.com/watch?v=aehKM1Ia_0I
- HM Passport Office:
  https://www.gov.uk/government/organisations/hm-passport-office
- Open Government Solutions:
  https://aws.amazon.com/government-education/open-government-solutions/

Hashtags: #AWSSummit #DigitalGovernment #PublicSector #AWS #CloudComputing #DigitalTransformation #UserCentric

Enterprise Transformation and Cost Optimization with Intel

The AWS Summit Ottawa 2022 featured a 50-minute session, "How to Launch Enterprise Transformation & Optimize Cost," sponsored by Intel. Moderated by Maria Ellis, AWS Senior Manager for Canadian Public Sector Partners, the panel included Andre LeDuc, AWS Business Development Manager; Kevin Grimes, Public Sector Amazon Business; and Graham Denny, Deputy CIO of Athabasca University (AU). The session explored how AU's cloud migration, leveraging AWS and Intel's partnership, achieved agility, cost savings, and Innovation. This post examines the session's insights, focusing on cloud economics, building a business case, and AU's transformation journey.

Understanding Cloud Economics

Maria Ellis introduced cloud economics, emphasizing its role across the cloud journey. Unlike traditional IT, where organizations over-provision hardware to meet forecasted demand, cloud offers elasticity, scaling resources to match actual needs. Ellis illustrated this with a chart comparing traditional (over-provisioned) capacity to cloud's dynamic scaling, reducing waste. Gartner and McKinsey note 50% excess capacity in traditional setups, a common issue for public sector clients. Cloud eliminates this, enabling pay-as-you-go models, reducing costs, and accelerating innovation by bypassing cumbersome procurement cycles.

Ellis highlighted that cloud necessitates new financial and operational models. Traditional IT budgeting is rigid, involving long approval and installation processes, leading to over-provisioning and stifled experimentation. Cloud aligns finance and technology teams, shortening cycles and fostering agility. Andre LeDuc expanded on this, introducing the AWS Cloud Value Framework, derived from 1,500 customer migrations. The framework identifies four pillars: cost savings (27% average reduction), staff productivity (58% more VMs per admin), operational resilience (57% less downtime), and business agility (38% faster time-to-market). These metrics guide organizations in quantifying cloud benefits.

Building a Robust Business Case

LeDuc outlined five steps for a cloud business case: discovery, landscape mapping, forecasting, comparing total cost of ownership (TCO), and migration cost analysis. Discovery involves inventorying current infrastructure using tools like AWS Migration Evaluator to assess utilization. Landscape mapping right-sizes workloads, leveraging cloud elasticity. Forecasting incorporates AWS savings plans, reducing costs up to 75%. TCO ensures an apples-to-apples comparison with on-premises costs, while migration costs account for dual-running and training, offset by AWS programs like Migration Evaluator.

A comprehensive TCO requires consolidating data across teams—network, hardware, and facilities—often fragmented in organizations. LeDuc emphasized that incomplete data risks rejection by executives. AWS's methodology, supported by market data, simplifies this, enabling holistic cost forecasts. Ellis noted that while cost savings dominate, including productivity, resilience, and agility metrics strengthens the case. AU's case, as Denny later shared, exemplifies this, achieving significant savings by avoiding hardware purchases and optimizing utilization.

Athabasca University's Transformation Journey

Graham Denny detailed AU's cloud migration, making it Canada's first post-secondary institution with 100% production workloads on AWS. AU, an online university with 44,000 students across 92 countries, faced a complex legacy environment. Discovery involved scanning hardware, software, and ROI with multiple tools, ensuring a clear baseline. Working with AWS, AU built a business case evaluating cloud economics, TCO, and growth costs. The decision to migrate without optimizing on-premises minimized disruption, prioritizing student and staff experience.

AU's migration yielded tangible benefits. By avoiding $1.8–2.5 million annual server purchases, AU reduced IT costs significantly. Elasticity eliminated over-provisioning, with systems scaling dynamically. Tools like AWS Cost Explorer and Trusted Advisor optimized spending, while reserved instances saved 21.4%. AU's "Integrated Learning Environment" initiative modernized operations, retiring outdated systems. Collaboration with AWS Professional Services and Managed Services enhanced efficiency, and mandatory AWS training upskilled staff, fostering resilience and agility.

Collaboration with Amazon Business and Intel

Kevin Grimes highlighted Amazon Business's role in AU's transformation, emphasizing a "One Amazon" approach integrating AWS and Amazon Business. Launched in Canada in 2019, Amazon Business addresses public sector procurement challenges, offering a controlled marketplace with business pricing and bulk discounts. AU began using Amazon Business for COVID supplies in 2020, evolving to IT and traditional supplies like books. Tools like QuickSight, built on AWS, provide procurement insights, enhancing efficiency. Intel's Pat Gelsinger underscored the AWS-Intel partnership, from EC2's scalability to AI enhancements via SageMaker, enabling AU's robust cloud infrastructure.

The session concluded with Denny emphasizing that migration is a journey, not a one-time event. AU continues optimizing, leveraging AWS tools and training to reduce risks and enhance student experiences. The collaborative approach—AWS, Amazon Business, Intel—demonstrates how integrated solutions drive transformation while controlling costs.

Links:

- AWS Summit Ottawa 2022 Video:
  https://www.youtube.com/watch?v=B2YEYT403lw
- Athabasca University: https://www.athabascau.ca/
- Amazon Business: https://www.amazon.ca/business

Hashtags: #AWSSummit #CloudEconomics #PublicSector #AWS #Intel #DigitalTransformation #CostOptimization

www.ingramcontent.com/pod-product-compliance
Lightning Source LLC
LaVergne TN
LVHW010040070326
832903LV00071B/4534